UNSPOKEN Languages

Making your beliefs speak for you.

BY ROBIN AYERS

Acclaim for

Making your beliefs speak for you.

"A powerful read. Robin puts into words what so many of us are searching for and intuitively know…that we have the power to control our destiny. I recommend this book for anyone looking for effective tools and techniques to help them achieve their dreams."

- **Quincy C. Newell**
Executive Vice President & General Manager
Code Black Films / a Lionsgate Company

Publisher's note: This is a work of fiction. Names, characters, places, and incidents either are the product of the author's imagination or are used fictitiously. Any resemblance to actual events, locales, or persons, living or dead, is entirely coincidental.

Printed in the United States of America

Line edited, formatted, and interior design by Kristen Corrects, Inc.

Cover art design by Phoenix White I Emkron Studios

First edition published 2016

10 9 8 7 6 5 4 3 2 1

Ayers, Robin

Unspoken languages: Making Your Beliefs Speak For You/ Robin Ayers

p. cm.

ISBN-13: 978-0-9980936-0-4

ISBN-10: 0998093602

Credits

Photography (Phoenix White)

Book Cover & Format (Phoenix White Emkron Studios, www.emkron.net)

Editor (Kristen Hamilton, www.kristencorrects.com)

Dedication

Dedication

I dedicate this book to my daughters Madison and Brooklyn. There are so many messages and lessons that I want you to learn from me but this is by far one of the most important. I had a dream one night that God spoke to me specifically about life. He said, "Life is all about belief." Everything you believe will manifest itself and you two know more than anyone that I am living proof of that. I believe in the power that our beliefs have, and Madi and Brook, I need for you to believe that as well. Believe that everything you desire is possible to obtain. Intentional belief is a force and after reading this book I pray that you apply it to your own life. I love you more than words can explain. As much as I want to believe that I teach you so much about life, just know that you both give me life lessons that are priceless. Thank you for teaching me, pulling from me, and pushing me to be greater each day than the day prior.

Love unconditionally,

– Mommy

Table of Contents

06   **Dedication**

10   **Authors Note**

16   **Introduction**

21   **Chapter 01** | *Inhale, Exhale*

43   **Chapter 02** | *What's Your Order?*

55   **Chapter 03** | *Get In The Game*

65   **Chapter 04** | *Borrow Confidence*

77   **Chapter 05** | *Jump! Your Wings Will Grow*

89   **Chapter 06** | *Assist In Your Own Rescue*

99   **Chapter 07** | *Belief Works For Your Or Against You*

111 **Chapter 08** | *Beyond 5 Miles*

121 **Chapter 09** | *When The Rain Falls*

133 **Chapter 10** | *So You Believe, Now What?*

143 **Chapter 11** | *Birds of a Feather*

152 **Acknowledgments**

Authors Note

For years I've had the unbreakable, unfathomable support of you, my friends and my family, both close and extended. It was you who had given me the confidence that I had a voice and a purpose to speak to the masses. I am just a girl from Milwaukee, Wisconsin who fervently believed she heard from God over thirty years ago that would change her life forever.

I grew up in a tumultuous environment. I don't remember laughing or smiling much at all. I was quiet and almost afraid of speaking so I observed and listened a lot. My father was tough, strict and stern. Everyone in our house feared him, including me even though I was a small child. My mother who was doing everything she could to stay above water, attended school, work, and cared for her three young children while continuously trying to please my father. I don't want to paint him out as though he was an evil person because he wasn't.

My father is actually a charming, funny and loving man but back then he was abusing drugs and alcohol, which contributed to his short tempers and abusive ways. As an adult I have forgiven my father and I've made a conscious decision to try understanding him and all he dealt with in his past.

With all of the physical abuse and chaos that went on in our household, I often found myself feeling dark and alone. Usually my older brother and older sister were somewhere nearby but on this particular day I distinctly remember being by myself.

As I knelt on my knees looking out the window in my bedroom, nothing in particular kept my attention but I could feel the warmth of the sun shining on my shoulders. Although I could never remember anyone talking to me about God, I was quite sure that at that moment He was graciously introducing Himself to me. It was almost like He was hiding in the sun.

He began speaking to me in a way that was calm and peaceful and that I could clearly understand. I was no more than four years old, but I wasn't afraid. I was at peace. I heard Him clearly.

He said; "things won't always be this way. It gets much better. I am going to set you apart and make you different. I will use you to help them."

Leila, Me, Arthur

A few years after

that life-defining moment, I began having daily dreams that I was a bird. I would carry my family members on my back and fly them from harm into a place of safety. In my dreams I would also pick up random people and fly them to safety. I never told anyone about all of this until I was much older but I've always held onto it. I didn't place a significant value on it until I started to see a pattern in my life when I was around eighteen years old. I would have conversations with people and they'd say things like, "Robin you should consider being a counselor because your advice is so good," or "You make me feel so comfortable when I talk to you. I feel like I can share my whole life's story with you."

As I grew older I would recall the message that God gave me when I was a kid. Pieces of the puzzle were revealing in time exactly what He meant back then. Naturally I began to speak what was in my heart. I never spoke for acclaim or acknowledgment but only for truth. My truth happened to resonate with your truths. Before long, I knew God was using me just like he said He would. I was fulfilling my purpose and you all have helped me to realize that.

Thank you for hearing my heart and seeing me for who I am and accepting what I share on a daily basis. This book is alive because of you, and God of course! I pray that this book touches whom it's meant for and it's applied to your life for a greater growth than you've ever known.

My deepest love,

Robin

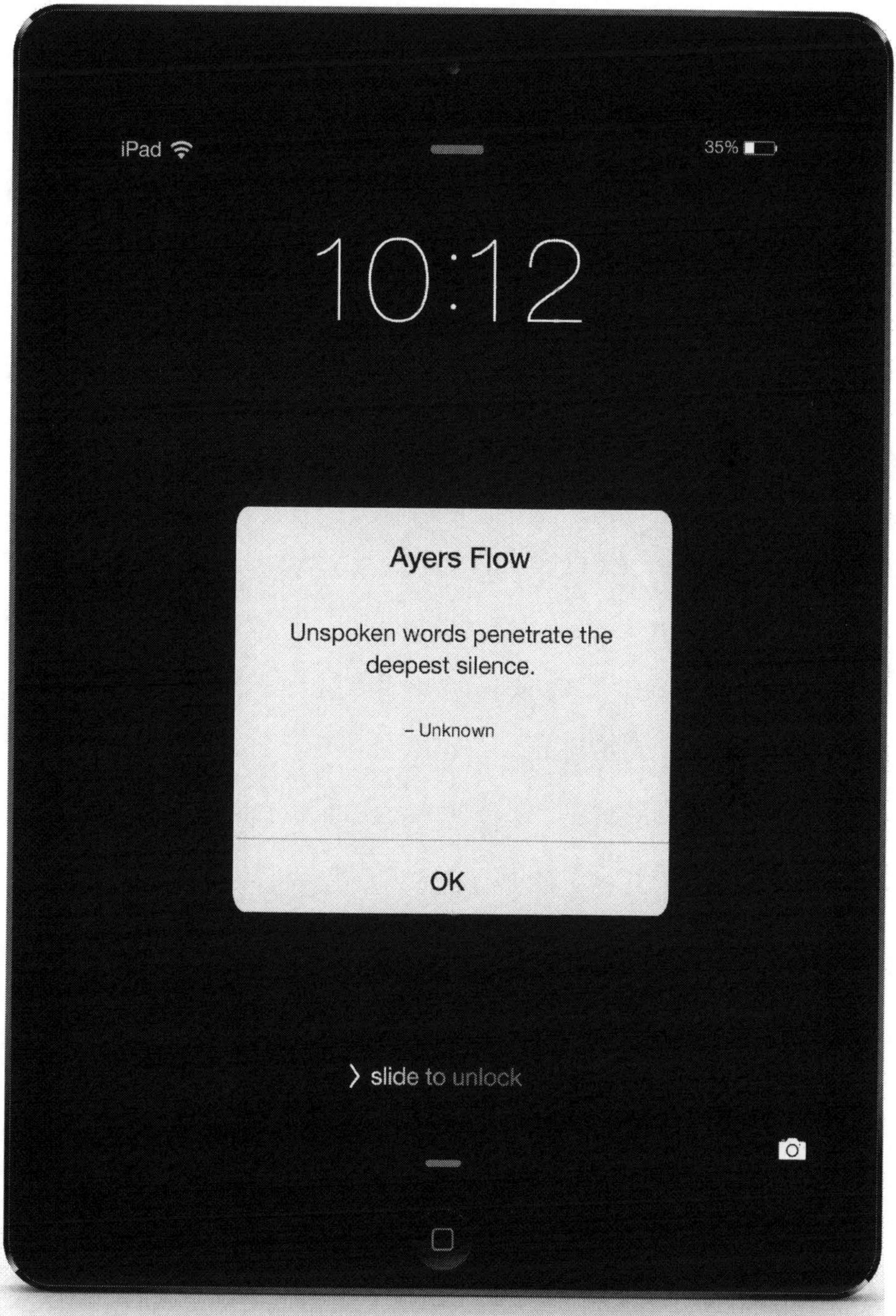

iPad 📶 10:12 35%

Ayers Flow

Unspoken words penetrate the deepest silence.

– Unknown

OK

❯ slide to unlock

Introduction

There's a man who is a drug addict. He went to a party and started having a conversation with another man. Something drew them to each other and neither of them mentioned their pasts but somehow they both understood that the other was on drugs of some kind. Little did they know they actually had the same substance abuse problem— but that never came up in conversation at all. Maybe they saw it in each other's demeanor. Maybe it was the physical features that they both felt were so familiar and identified with, but they clearly had an undeniable connection. They exchanged numbers and became good friends and yes, eventually they began doing drugs together.

When I heard this story, I thought, *how very interesting* that there is a language that they both understood but neither had to verbally speak it in order to communicate to other. Somehow they just knew!

Isn't that the case with so many things? Don't we all speak languages that are unspoken that other people who communicate that same language understands? If you see me walk into a fast food restaurant and I stand in line, you'll automatically assume that I am hungry, right? That, in and of itself, is a language that is unspoken. If I am in my college classroom diligently working and I see you in the same classroom diligently working, I assume that you are trying to graduate at the top of your class the same way that I am. There are tons of languages that are communicated everyday without speaking one word.

Belief, like so many other examples, is a language that we speak directly to God as well as to the universe. Your belief is always speaking whether you know it or not. It says whether you believe in yourself or you don't. It says whether you believe something will work out or it won't. It is always working in sync with you and your mind both consciously and unconsciously, which is why it's so important to become aware of it. This is something you've heard before. But I want to go a step further. I want you to become aware of *intentional* belief. That is when you align everything inside of yourself with this particular belief of yours. Putting your belief in forward motion towards something is being intentional about it. Intentional belief is deciding the way in which you want it to go to work for you. It is for a purpose and it is on purpose. It is an unstoppable force that has no choice but to grant you what you've believed for. Though beliefs are considered intangible, just like spoken words, they carry a relentless power that maneuvers throughout the universe in a way that most of us wouldn't understand. Some things are unseen but quite undeniable such as the air we breathe. No one alive could deny that breathing invisible air is what keeps us alive.

If we understand the power that our intentional beliefs have and understand that eventually they manifest, we can begin to create the lives the way that we want. You are reading this book—and I believe that this isn't by accident. You are manifesting great things in your life, and your belief is one of them. William Arthur Ward said it best: "Believe while others are doubting." There are many people who won't understand this very simple concept. Many people will continue to doubt and feel like they are powerless in this world of mystique, but when you finish this book, you will know how to put your belief to great use for your life!

7:22

Ayers Flow

Believe while others are
doubting.

– William Arthur Ward

OK

> slide to unlock

CHAPTER ONE

Inhale, Exhale

Why is it that you wake up in the morning and go to the bathroom to brush your teeth, you turn the faucet on knowing that water will come rushing out? You don't give a second thought about it because your belief is that it will surely come on, unless by some chance the bill wasn't paid. When you flip the light switch on, your expectation is that the electricity will ignite the bulb in the ceiling to light up the room—right? I mean, why wouldn't it? If you've done your part in paying your dues, it is your right to have the water flowing through the faucet and the light to brighten the room. If it's that simple for us to believe in the "powers that be" behind our electricity and water, why can't we believe that the powers of God aren't the same or even more powerful?

Listen, I am by no means some guru who has mystically figured out the meaning of life. I have not had some inexplicable out-of-body experience that put me in the presence of God. As you read earlier, I am just a girl who was gifted with a message when she was four years old and has since learned a few things about how God works in our lives. Through my ongoing relationship with belief, I've figured out that consistency doesn't lie with me; instead it lies with the universe. What I mean is that no matter what you choose to believe, the universe will always be consistent in bringing that thing to you, both negative things and positive things.

My parents sent me to California at age four to live with my grandparents until my siblings finished school. The plan was to drive out to meet up with me in Carson, CA where my grandparents lived. When I moved to California, I didn't know that it was considered the land of opportunity. I didn't know that the famous Hollywood, CA was in my backyard. I remember always seeing those huge spotlights crossing each other in the sky. I had no idea what the lights meant or where it was coming from, but I was drawn to them each night. Somehow, I innately knew that it had something to do with the entertainment industry. The desire to be in the midst of it all was heavy on my spirit, even at such a young age. I would watch movies and TV shows where the camera would pan upward and catch glimpses of the palm trees against blue skies and for me, it represented possibilities. I was now included in that possibility living in California. I loved seeing palm trees sway back and forth in the wind. It was just something about it that felt freeing!

When I was in Milwaukee, there was a dark cloud in our house all of the time. The cloud was in the form of fear, intimidation and anxiety. Fortunately I was able to turn to television as an escape for myself. I would watch cartoons a lot as well entertainment shows like "Solid Gold" and "Soul Train". I would zone out completely when those things came on because it was a way to temporarily take a vacation in my mind. I wanted to be wherever they were in that television. I wanted to have something to do with it. There was an incredibly safe feeling that I had when I watched television.

As I sit here over thirty years later, I am in awe that my belief has brought me to the place I am now. I am literally living my dreams covering red carpet events, directly in the center of Hollywood. I am in the midst of "lights, camera, and action"! Little did I know that the desire for entertainment for me wasn't about the glitz and glam but it was to have a platform for my true purpose: inspiring others. I'm no different than most of you, but I understand that if I consistently dreamt of the most beautiful life and I believed I could live it, I certainly would. In fact, in this very moment I am living the very life that I dreamed of long ago. I am happy, I am grateful, and I laugh a lot. I tuck my kids into bed every night and I get up every morning and greet them along with my husband, Robbie. In my household you can expect to hear "I love you" about fifty times between all four people who live here. I don't know if that's overkill or not, but I like it that way. I like it a lot! We don't argue. That's right, I said it. We do not argue. Sure, we have had quite a few disagreements, but that doesn't mean we have to get loud and argue about them. Robbie and I had our fair share of listening to chaotic arguments from our parents when we were growing up, so we decided that we wouldn't be that way with our own kids. I acknowledge that my beliefs have gotten me to where I am. Despite my past childhood experiences, I have overcome them knowing the power that lies within me. We are not products of our environment if we don't want to be. We are the products of our belief system—point blank.

Robbie, Madison, Brooklyn, Me

Let's try something! Relax and take a deep breath. Close your eyes for a moment. Now acknowledge your presence by recognizing that you're alive. Acknowledge that out of all the people in the world, you were specially thought of when you were created. Inhale all of the possibilities, favor, blessings, goodness, healthiness, encouragement, positivity and support that belong to you. Now exhale all doubts, fear, worry, guilt, self-pity, and concerns that do not belong to you. When you exhale, visually imagine blowing it all away from you and when you inhale, visually pull it into you. This is a practice that I've discovered has worked for me when I'm just getting my day started. I love to start my day with the possibilities in life and claim that I have extreme favor to achieve them all. If this doesn't work for you, alter it to make it your own. Find something that makes you feel like you are triumphant everyday, because you certainly are.

Here is another practice of mine that I want to share with you. I often drive to a hill or mountain where I have a good view of the valley below. Usually my scenery is overlooking trees, buildings, houses and skylines. I remind myself that I have dominion over all of these things. I fill my chest with air and confidence that I am Robin Ayers and I am one amazingly powerful individual.

You should try this exercise and remember to be confident in who you are. Remember that there was only one of you born in the world and you have a definitive purpose for being here. You are extremely powerful!

If you have children, doesn't it feel amazing to watch them walk in confidence? You created them so you want them to boldly claim their identity and be proud of it, right? If you don't have kids quite yet, imagine how proud your parents are when you represent them the right way and show the world what your family is made of. This is the way God has to feel when we know our importance. When we walk around confidently and proud of whom we belong to, our creator wants to grant us more things that we can be even more proud about!

I don't want this to be just another book that you begin to read and then stop. I want you to be open to hearing the truth about yourself, the truth about the power you were born with. I'm not professing to know it all, nor do I want to because nothing is more beautiful than continuously learning and expanding the mind. I'm simply telling you about such a power that, if applied, can be one of the greatest gifts that you can ever experience—and hopefully even pass it along to someone else some day.

Although this topic is an unspoken language, it certainly knows how to communicate and move effectively throughout the universe. I say, "move" because it does indeed travel. The power of belief can be applied to all things in life including belief in other people and for other people.

If everything is about belief, then why doesn't everyone have what he or she is yearning for? American author and motivational speaker Jim Rohn says it this way, "What is easy to do is easy not to do." I couldn't have thought of a better way to say it myself. Even when people know the correct ways to get things done, it's usually such a small task that it's easy enough not to get it done.

For example, I know that the best way to keep my kitchen sink clean is to wash dishes as I go along throughout my day. Use a fork, wash the fork. Simple, right? Well, as simple as that may sound, it's easy to say, "It's just a measly little fork. I'll just set it down in the sink because it won't make a big difference." True, the fork is not the big deal, but once I set the dirty fork down, I'll want to set the dirty bowl down next, then the dirty plate, and next the dirty cup. Before you know it, there's a sink full of dirty dishes when it all should've started with cleaning one little fork.

The concept of belief is much the same way. If we consciously believed for the things we want, we could format our lives into a beautiful dream for ourselves. But it's easy to just let all kinds of thoughts take over our minds, just like allowing the dishes to take over the sink. We often get caught up living by default. We live day-by-day and let life dictate our minds rather than put our minds in control to affect our lives.

I'm sure that at some point in time in your life you've heard the cliché phrase to believe in yourself. I too, have heard that phrase many times, but the problem was that no one was willing to explain exactly what that meant. It was like all of the other phrases I had heard before that no one really cared to explain to me. "Whatever you do, don't mess up your credit." "Don't have sex until you're married." "You can do anything if you just believe in yourself."

These were all things that should have been self-explanatory but they weren't. Not in the least. When I was younger I promised myself that I would explain to my future children exactly what these things meant. I would break it down to whoever had an ear to listen. "Believe in yourself" is cliché, but there is more to it than just that. Let's take it all the way back to the basics where it all started from—the Bible!

Genesis 1:26:

"And God said, Let us make man in our image, after our likeness: and let them have dominion over the fish of the sea, and over the fowl of the air, and over the cattle, and over all the earth, and over every creeping thing that crept upon the earth. So God created man in his own image, in the image of God created he him; male and female created he them."

When I really began to understand this scripture in Genesis, I viewed my role in this world completely different. Most people don't understand the power that they have been born with.

Let me see if I can explain this so it's easier to understand. There are two small pebbles. The first pebble gets thrown into the ocean and because it knows how small it is, the pebble says, "This ocean is going to swallow me alive. Look how powerful this ocean is. It's tossing me back and forth." The second pebble gets thrown in and it also knows its size. This pebble says, "I'm so small in comparison to this ocean but look how strong I am. Watch me make ripple waves in this water."

Both of these pebbles are the same and both were thrown into the same water, but they had very different belief systems.

I've always had the mentality that I was the pebble that caused the ocean to have the ripple effect. That is one powerful pebble. One that understands just because you're so small in the midst of a mighty body of water, you're still effective. You still have a say-so. You still have power and you can move the ocean! If God said we were made in His image and likeness, how powerful then are we? We have been given the gift of Godliness. We have the power to speak things into existence and they become! I get chills every time I think about that! We have the power over things on this earth because that's the way He put it into place!

Yes, our world is very large and you are but one individual but you are an individual whom was created by God! Not on accident. Not by mistake. But on purpose, with a purpose to fulfill those desires He instilled in you. Those desires will be effective in serving a purpose for the greater good and will ultimately help someone in this world, so you are doing yourself and God a disservice by not knowing your power and walking in it.

I've found that more than *saying*, "I believe," there is an unmatched force when you *do* believe. When you believe that you are created in God's image, you'll see that you have been dealt the same power He has. When you believe that you can speak things into existence, you'll see that those things will show up in your life because you demanded that they do so. When you believe that you can utilize those things to better your life and accomplish the things that you desire, you will see that you'll have all those things and more. Now that, in my opinion, is the breakdown of the cliché phrase "believe in yourself."

If you are willing, take this ride with me to see how I developed a better understanding for myself. Hopefully you will also get a better grasp and understanding of the

Unspoken Language of Belief and begin to implement it in your own life.

Get Back In the
Drivers Seat

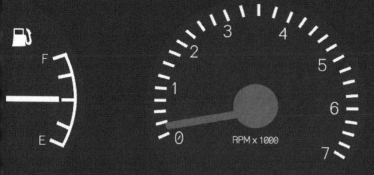

Have you ever taken a taxi ride? When you get in the car the driver asks you for your destination. Even though you give the driver the address, it is up to him or her to decide the path they will take to get you there. You can't control the route they take and you can't control the speed they go.

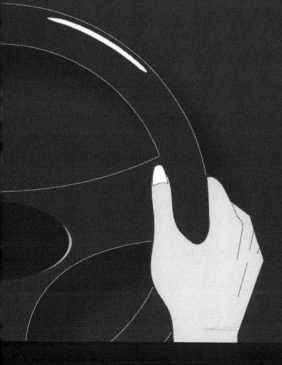

So many of us have become passengers in our lives. I'm asking you to believe in yourself again and get back in the driver's seat. Have faith that you will maneuver through the traffic of the world. Understand that there are some potholes and bumps along the way, but if you know where you are headed, you can get there! Like the small pebble, you must believe that you are strong enough.

Name a few areas that you've allowed someone to take over the wheel for you. Then list the ways that you will commit to taking your control back. Remember, God created you in His image. You've got this!!

Inhale, Exhale

EXERCISE

Nugget Notes

....

....

....

....

....

....

....

....

....

....

....

iPad 📶   82% 🔋

7:14

Ayers Flow

If you see it in your mind, you'll
hold it in your hand.

– Bob Proctor

OK

❯ **slide** to unlock

CHAPTER TWO

What's your Order?

On Twitter I used to follow Tyrese, a famous singer and actor who is also well known as a motivational guy on social media. Years ago he asked his followers what we believed for that year. Since he was also following me, I had the opportunity to direct message him my answer. I told him that one of my goals was to have a sit down conversation with him. I wanted to pick his brain about certain things in his life and how he achieved them. Well lo and behold, he actually responded! He told me that he wasn't able to sit down with me but he could call me on the phone and have a conversation.

I was so quick to respond to him with my number. I wasn't really prepared to talk to him like I wanted to but I still took the opportunity knowing it may not come around again. He called and our conversation helped change my entire outlook on life. He asked me several founding questions such as who I was and what I did for a living. He also wanted to know where I wanted to go in life. At that time my goals were a lot different than they are now but the principles he gave me still apply to this day.

Tyrese gave me great advice about career moves and how to become a skillful networker, but the most powerful thing he said to me still applies—it was about belief! He said, "If you go to a restaurant and place an order for steak, does the waiter bring you chicken?" I said, "No, the waiter brings you what you ordered. Steak." Tyrese continued explaining that life is pretty much the same way. We have a certain expectation and belief that when we place an order for something at a restaurant, we will receive exactly what we ordered…but for some reason, people waver in their beliefs when it comes to their "orders" or prayers that they put into the universe for God to hear and answer. This resonated with me. Does this resonate with you? What is your order that you've placed into the universe? It will surely bring you what you've asked for.

"The Setback Is Actually A Setup"

A man named Koran Bolden worked a nine to five job but wasn't very happy there. He was grateful for his position and being able to bring home a steady check for his family but he also believed heavily that there was much more to life than what he was living. He came to the conclusion that he wanted to become an entrepreneur and build a music studio in the mall in his hometown. This would be the perfect place where the inner city youth would come to be creative and expressive, all while creating music that they loved. He estimated that he would need fifteen thousand dollars to start his business but he had no idea where this money would come from considering he didn't make much money at the job he was working. That didn't stop his belief. He began to speak into existence the exact amount of money he needed for his business. He placed his order!

One day Koran came into work and had received an email from his employer that they were letting him go from the company! After getting through the initial shock and disappointment of being laid off, he continued to read the rest of the email. It stated that even though he was no longer going to have his job, they were giving him a severance package. Guess how much they were sending him away with? That's right! Fifteen thousand dollars! That was the exact amount he needed to start his business and subsequently, he did just that! Koran and his wife built a successful music studio business and it was all based on his belief that he would receive the money he needed regardless of his circumstances! He placed his "order" in the universe and he was given exactly what he asked for.

After speaking with Tyrese, just like Koran, I immediately began to put this theory to the test. Every chance I got I would ask God (in the same way that I would place an order), for boldness or clarity or something specific that I was believing for and that became my set expectation without wavering. I wanted to see for myself if we really do have a power that is unspoken.

I've heard my Pastor Fred L. Hodge, Jr. talk about the fact that we are spiritual beings having a natural experience and if that were the case, I needed to see if my spirit of belief could communicate with the spirit of God.

It makes plenty of sense that the unseen can directly communicate with each other. No wonder our words can be used as a weapon. Think about it. When you've had arguments in your life and someone says something deliberately to hurt your feelings, it feels like a weapon that they've used against you. You feel the pain of those words in your spirit because they have communicated with one another. On the other hand, if someone pays you a compliment, you smile or laugh because their words have effectively communicated positively with your spirit. So that was the plan for me. Use my unseen words, my unseen prayer, and my unseen belief to communicate with that which is also un-seen—God and the universe. If there were something I really desired, I'd put my entire belief behind it and claim it to be mine. I sent positive vibrations out to the universe and let it be known that it was mine. I would take steps toward the thing I desired and before long, I would possess it and it would serve as confirmation for me all over again. To this day, even though I'm a lot more confident in my power of achieving the things I want in life, I still find myself proving the unspoken language power to myself just to be sure that it works.

Recently I pulled into an underground parking lot that's usually filled with cars because of its prime location in Hollywood. However, this particular day was even more jam-packed because of a major event that was happening. It was the world premiere screening for a Walt Disney animation film with some pretty big stars expected to show up. That meant that almost every parking spot was filled in this underground parking garage.

I was in a hurry to park because I was working as the red carpet correspondent for this screening and I needed to check in and get my media badge. When I entered the parking lot I spoke out loud, "Okay

God, you know I need my favorite parking spot. I need a parking spot close to the escalators. Thank you in advance."

I set out to find my spot. It seemed as though I was driving in circles looking for someone to pull out of their spot so I could pull right in behind them. As I looked at the time getting closer to my deadline to check in, I started to question my power and myself (doubt). Does this still work for me? Is God mad at me? These were the thoughts running through my mind as I continued to drive. Then I had a reve-latory moment—a "Robin" moment where I put aside my doubt and became optimistic again (intentional belief). This absolutely still works for me! This is a principle no matter who you are, or what you feel you've done wrong. It works for everybody! I reassured myself and put my confidence back into the unspoken language principal: my belief!

I drove around one more time and like clockwork, a car pulls out of the parking spot directly next to the main door where the escala-tors were! YES GOD! Principles don't change, people do! People talk themselves out of their own blessings many times. The things you've believed for are happening all around you but if your eyes aren't open to seeing them, you'll miss it.

Correspondant

Can I take your order?

At this exact moment become certain of who you are! If I asked you your name, you would tell me. You wouldn't doubt it. You wouldn't flinch. You would say it with absolute certainty. If I asked you for your address or your phone number, you'd recite it as though it's ingrained in your mind. Right now, I need you to be that sure of whom you are. Remember, you are a force and when you speak to the universe, it listens but most importantly, it replies. What do you believe for? What is your request? Be unapologetic about placing your order. Keep in mind that the waiter brings you exactly what you ask for.

So here you are. It is time to believe in your power. Write down what you currently believe for. There is no room to doubt it. There is no room to question whether or not you'll receive it. There is no room for logic. Those will all have their own times in your life, but now is not the time. This moment is simply about pure belief. After you've written down your order(s), say them aloud. Repeat them. Breathe them in. Allow them to find a comfortable place inside of you. It belongs there. At the end of this book you'll find room to write down any testimonies or proof stories you have.

Universal Order Form	
1	
2	
3	
4	
5	
6	
7	
8	
9	
10	

11:30

Ayers Flow

The game of life has two participants. Spectators and players. Pick one.

– Unknown

OK

> slide to unlock

CHAPTER THREE

Get in the Game

When I started writing this book I thought about all the people who are just like me, people who have a tough beginning that's similar to mine or even worse off than mine. But I have to admit, I've seen and been through quite a bit and I often wonder, why am I not a statistic?

Isn't that what the world teaches us? They say that if you've been brought up in a home where your parents or older siblings hadn't gone to college, that you also will more than likely skip the college experience. They say that if you grew up in the ghetto, more than likely you won't make it out of the ghetto. So again, the question is why? Why am I not with a physically abusive man? Why am I not a drug addict? Why have I never gone to prison? Why do I live in a house full of laughter and love rather than drama and chaos? The simple answer is that I became a player in this game called life and belief was my fuel to win.

What if I told you that the day you were born was the day you made the team as a player in life? It's thought provoking, I'm sure. Most people succumb to the idea that they have seen too many negative things, been broken too long, and that they aren't strong enough to make themselves better. The easiest option becomes to settle with whatever is thrown your way and believe that you have to take a seat on the bench and watch the other players play the game. That is not the case and I don't want you to fall for that! My goal is to help you suit up, identify your opponent in life so that you know how to defeat it, play the game, score repeatedly, and ultimately win in the game also using belief as your fuel.

Have you ever gone to a real basketball or football game and you're in the stands shouting at the players because you're either excited with them or you're angry at the play that they made? It's interesting that we vicariously live through the players when we haven't contributed anything at all to the success of the game. The players put in their blood, sweat, and tears to win championship games but here we are shouting from afar because we agree or disagree with the play.

The energy on the sidelines is usually quite infectious and it's very lively because that's where the majority of the people are. I've seen fights break out because one bystander will make a remark about a player on the opposing team and another bystander gets offended. Both of these people have absolutely nothing do with the game other than they paid money to observe, yet they get so offended with one another that they're willing to go to blows over it. But haven't we seen these things happen in real life? Isn't there a tendency to get so involved in someone else's life that you're willing to get emotionally and sometimes physically uncomfortable if someone mentions anything bad about that person?

I'm sure you've seen it. They are the people who read blogs every day hoping to find out the juiciest gossip on their favorite celebrities. They are the people who watch the entertainment news, living through others who chose to go out and live their lives. These are the people that watch reality TV stars live glamorous lives dressed in designer clothes and driving fancy cars, but who are too afraid to go after their own dreams to achieve their own success. These people are the ones who believe in someone else's dream but afraid to believe in their own. Nothing is wrong with admiring reality stars. Nothing is wrong with admiring celebrities. Nothing is wrong with applauding people as they strive for greatness…but there are plenty of opportunities for everyone to be inspired by them and motivated to get their own. Motivation often comes from the belief that something is possible for you. If you believe with motivation, you'd play with a different kind of passion.

Instead of being motivated to live our own lives to the fullest, sometimes it's simply easier to live life through someone else's dream. It often feels good to dream a perfect scenario in our head, but the fear is, what if we pursue that dream and it's nothing like we thought? Sometimes just dreaming about something is more than enough for people.

It feels good in your mind. It's perfect in your mind. You can go to that place and daydream whenever you feel like doing it and nobody is there to ruin that perfect place. Sometimes the very thing that stops people from trying to really achieve that perfect dream is the fear that it won't end up the way they felt about it when it was just a dream. What if we fail at it or we find that we're terrible at it? Then we have to deal with the fear that we will be judged. Sometimes we may not even believe that we're good enough after failing at something. What if we succeed at it? Then we need to deal with the common fear that you will no longer be in your comfort zone. Everything around you will change. Success causes change. So, instead of participating, we stick to being spectators of the game. That is where we can comfortably participate without risking anything.

There are some people who actually step out of their comfort zone to create a new comfort zone. It is a difficult thing to do but it's possible if you consciously make the effort to change everyday.

I admire people who may not know anything about a particular subject—but rather than watch other people participate, they make a decision to learn everything there is to know and they begin to apply it. They may even become good or great at it, which is all the better! That is a person who has fully committed to believing that they are capable and that things can be different for them.

Lets Play!!!

A few years ago I decided to say yes to everything that presented itself as an opportunity. No matter what it was, if someone asked me to participate, I said yes as long as it wasn't harmful to my family or me. That gesture allowed me to really live life to its fullest. I want the same for you. It's time to get back in the game of life!

What are a few things you would try if you knew you would succeed? What are some things you would try if you couldn't get hurt doing them? What are some things you've always wanted to do but you didn't give yourself permission to try? What do you watch other people do that you wish you had the guts to participate in?

Within the next month, do at least two of the things you mention on your list. Watch how your belief ignites and catapults you into another level!

EXERCISE

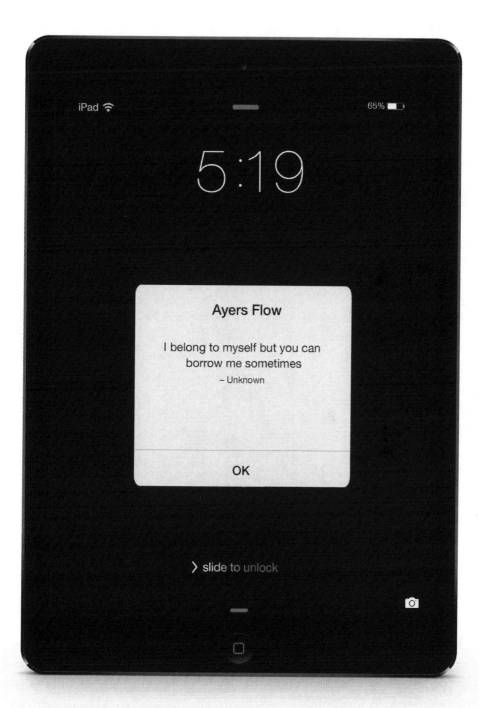

CHAPTER FOUR

Borrow Confidence

I was a smart girl but I didn't always show it in school. It was just that my study habits hadn't been set up from the very beginning. When I was a young child, my parents worked a lot so I was left to the care of my older sister and brother. My parents didn't realize that my siblings never did their homework, so that also became my pattern. Unfortunately, those habits followed me all throughout my academic career. My teachers often said, "Robin is a smart girl but she never does her homework."

When I reached high school I ditched a lot but never for the classes of Ms. Rita Hall. You knew Ms. Hall was coming from a mile away. She had pretty brown skin and she always wore individual box-braids in her hair. She had the most distinct voice on campus so you could hear her above the kids' voices in the hallways. Ms. Hall was my English teacher and cheerleading coach in high school. Any and everyone in that school could tell you that she was no joke! She didn't mess around with education. I felt lucky that she was my English teacher from ninth grade through my senior year because even though she was very strict, she also cared for her students. Ms. Hall was the type to curse you out then throw your backpack down the hallway if you misbehaved, and turn around and be the sweetest person in the world if you did what you were supposed to do.

At the time my best friend and I had Ms. Hall's classes together. We were given the nicknames Thelma and Louise because of our tight knit bond. She lived five minutes' walking distance from the school and oftentimes when we ditched we just went to her house to hang out.

Ms. Hall had taken a special interest in me. She saw more in me than I could see in myself at the time. She believed in my abilities and potential to be well rounded and educated, which explains why one day while ditching at my best friend's house, we heard the doorbell ring and we were both surprised because no one knew we were there—or so we thought.

She peaked out of the window and saw Ms. Hall standing at the front door! "Hide! It's Ms. Hall!" she screamed inside of a whisper. I hid in the pitch-black bedroom closet. The rhythm of my heartbeat became the soundtrack for that moment. My friend must not have been as afraid because she actually opened the front door. I heard the sound of footsteps pounding on the wood floor getting louder and louder and eventually drowning out the sound of my heartbeat. Instinct led that woman directly to the closet where I was. "Get out of this closet and go back to school Robin Davis!" she said sternly. I was mortified. All I could do is hang my head low and pray that she didn't call my mother to tell on me. I didn't realize it at the time but Ms. Hall usually went on a daily walk for her lunch break and on this particular day she had either seen me leaving or somehow just by instinct knew that I was ditching that day.

I never realized it at the time but Ms. Hall paid a lot of attention to me. She saw that I excelled when I applied myself in school and especially in her class. There was something special in me that she always recognized and according to her, she wouldn't ease up off of me until I pushed through. I needed Ms. Hall in those days. I didn't have the confidence in myself to make it through my senior year in high school. I was failing so many classes because of my ditching habits but Ms. Hall had unwavering confidence in me. She knew how bright I was. She knew how much potential I had and ultimately she believed I'd be somebody in life. I had just enough credits to make it through and graduate on time. I totally borrowed the confidence and belief that Ms. Hall and my parents had in me because I surely didn't have any of my own.

If you've ever heard the term "fake it 'til you make it," I passionately believe the same way about one's belief. Sometimes we need to temporarily borrow the belief and confidence that others have in us until we come into our own. Not everyone has grown up with people feeding positivity into him or her. Sometimes the environment that we grow up in is telling us that we won't be successful in life and that we should take a seat to watch the game while other people are actually playing it. That unfortunately becomes what people believe but that is not the truth!

Have you ever thought about what the biggest difference is in people who have a fervent drive to succeed and those who are complacent? Why does one person work hard toward something even without the evidence of the result being there while the other has already given up because they don't see the results yet? The answer is belief. The reason we give up on things we've started is we don't believe in the finished product or sometimes that we don't believe that it will ever get finished in the first place.

Coach Has Game

A newly retired NBA basketball coach decided that instead of staying home all day, he'd rather do something productive with his time. Although he coached professional ball players for most of his career, he wanted to coach at the local high school in his town. In that season this particular basketball team had one of the worst losing streaks in the history of the school. That didn't matter at all to the coach though. In fact, he wound up taking on that position without any pay. He wanted to see if he was able to raise the morale of the team who always seemed unhappy and unmotivated when it was time for them to play. Furthermore, he wanted to prove that with a simple correction of mindset, the outcome could mean a big payoff for the team.

Soon after the coach started working with the team, he asked the school's principle for a small budget to change their uniforms and paint the locker room. Since the coach had made plenty of connections while coaching in the NBA, he placed a few phone calls to friends in high-powered positions and got the team new drinking fountains in the gym and new basketballs to play with. With all the new attention the team received, the morale slowly lifted higher; however, things really began to skyrocket when the coach implemented affirmations before each practice and before each game. He would have the players repeat, "We are winners, we are champions, we are a team!" He would tell them how much he believed in them. He'd say that in all of his years of coaching professional basketball players, he had never seen as much heart as this young team played with.

To everyone's surprise, the team won game after game that season. Spectators came to each game to see what all of the buzz was about. Even the principle that hired the coach couldn't believe the results this team was having after such a downward spiral so he arranged an on-camera interview with each individual member of the team to get their point of view on their newfound success. When each person was asked what the difference was in that winning season versus the prior season, they all gave credit to the coach. Some players said that they had never had someone who believed in them the way their new coach did. Other players said that the coach helped to renew their minds when they renewed their environments and uniforms.

These players borrowed the confidence that their coach had in them and the end result was a new belief that they could actually win, which they ultimately accomplished.

Three Dimensions of Confidence

At all times, it's imperative to have three levels of confidence taking place in three types of relationships.

✓ Always have someone who you can borrow confidence from. They are more successful than you. They believe deeply in themselves. They believe in you and encourage you with words of wisdom.

✓ Have someone you can lend confidence to. These people need you in their life for guidance, tips, and confidence. They watch how you move and they become inspired by the way you live your life. Your belief ignites their belief and gains them more confidence.

✓ Have a peer who is like-minded with the same type of confidence as you. Together you sharpen each other's iron. They inspire you, but you also inspire them.

Think of these people. Become aware of them. Write them down! Confidence ignites belief and belief ignites the changes in your life.

EXERCISE

6:17

Ayers Flow

Even birds don't know they can
fly until they jump.

– Unknown

OK

> slide to unlock

CHAPTER FIVE

Jump, Your Wings Will Grow

Have you ever jumped off of a cliff without a harness or a parachute? Neither have I, but I can imagine that it'd probably be the scariest feeling on Earth. In mid air I'm sure a million thoughts would run through your mind including regret, doom, and even hope that your outcome would still be favorable.

That can describe the many thoughts and feelings that can go through your mind when you step out to try anything new. You may be jumping out on faith to start a new business. Perhaps it's a new relationship that you're feeling the desire to try. Going back to school, buying a house, moving to another city or state—these are all life experiences that require you to jump. However, when you jump, something awesome happens; you grow wings on your way down! Those wings may come in the form of someone who "magically" appeared to help you out with the exact information you needed. Maybe your wings come in the form of an unexpected check in the mail that came right in time to help you out of your bind. Exciting to think about right? It could be the thing you need most but you would never know what your wings look like until you jump.

Sometimes my kids and I feed the ducks at a lake near our house. It's awesome to see how they all swarm around us when we have food to give them. One thing I noticed is that on the outside majority of the ducks look alike. Most of them are brown with beige spots and others are all white. All of them are beautiful but all of the ducks are unique in their own way. When they spread their wings they each have the most astounding colors inside. This one has white and blue stripes, while that one has purple colored feathers sprouting out. Simply beautiful! I had never seen that before but it was a reminder that you don't know what your wings will bring until you spread them wide. Just like the ducks, your wings are also unique and won't look like anyone else's. Your life is specifically designed for you and that is the faith that you need to have when it's time to jump outside of your comfort zone.

Belief is just like faith. Faith is a strong unshakable belief in something especially without proof or evidence of it. There are so many things in life that require us to have faith in order to succeed at it. When we begin working out and exercising our body and go on a thirty-minute run around the neighborhood, we have already begun to burn calories but there is no evidence that we are losing any fat. We just have to believe that if we continuously exercise that we will see the weight loss.

Imagine you're standing at a red light ready to cross the street. Usually there is a signal button that you can push to send the message that there is a pedestrian who is waiting to cross. When you push the button, does the light automatically become green? No, there is a process—we just don't know what that process is because it's unseen to us. There are probably wires, receptors, and machines that need to receive the message that there is someone waiting to cross the light so that the red light can eventually become yellow, then red for the automobiles to stop. That exact scenario is what it is like to have faith. Just because we believe or pray for something doesn't mean that it will automatically appear that very moment or even that very day. There is a process to the things we believe for. There are unseen energies and frequencies and wires being crossed in ways that are unseen but are taking place on your behalf because you've "pushed the button." You have to be willing to continue doing the work and stay the course while the light turns green in order to get what you've asked for.

"Even birds don't know they can fly until they jump," and it will be the same way with us. We don't know what our future has in store for us. There may be new people, new business opportunities, and new relationships all waiting on our arrival but if you never take the leap of faith to get out there, you'll never know.

Don't allow fear or comfort to disable you to live your life to the fullest. Comfort, in my opinion, is the single worst enemy of faith. Comfort is playing it safe, and by playing it safe you stay in a box and fail to take risks that will cause you to grow. Faith, on the other hand is stepping out into the unknown and whole-heartedly believing that the universe will bring you what you desire. There is a big difference. When you jump out on faith, you've consciously decided to believe. When you decide, you become a force!

Although I believe in jumping, I also believe that we need wisdom when doing so. Preparation is the key. You still need to map out a plan and have mini goals to reach your destination but you can't get stuck there. That is why most people never realize their dreams. They get stuck at the edge of the cliff but never jump because of a fear of the unknown. There certainly is a real fear that every human being on the planet faces. It's understandable. Being afraid is natural and healthy in my opinion. It serves as a barometer of how you're feeling when certain things arise, but the challenge to overcome your fear should be accepted.

"You miss 100% of the shots you don't take." −Wayne Gretzky

I love an amazing Zen quote that says, "When the student is ready the teacher shall appear." When all the preparation is complete and you've figured out your plan, it is time to jump out. Once that happens, the teacher (or wings) will appear.

I've seen real stories of people who never leave their home because of fear. There is a fear of change that will cause them to remain in the comfort zone of where they live. They want to control their circumstances and life as much as possible. They know they can wake up, turn on the same television channels, eat whatever is in the refrigerator and live happily because it's a controlled environment.

The old adage says that at the end of your life, you'll regret more of the chances you didn't take than the ones you did take. Life is to be lived and you're alive today.

These are a few examples of people who have jumped out on faith. Even though they experienced failure originally, their wings eventually grew!

> **High-end fashion designer Vera Wang** was once an ice skater. When that didn't pan out, she went to work for Vogue magazine. After sixteen years with Vogue, she was not up for the editor-in-chief position so she left the company to become the head designer of her own brand. "Don't be afraid of failing. I think not trying is worse than failing. Have the courage to try." – Vera Wang

> **Arianna Huffington, Founder and editor-in-chief of The Huffington Post,** wrote a book that was rejected by 36 publishers. She states that failure is not the opposite of success. Failure is the stepping-stone to success.

> **Billionaire entrepreneur Sara Blakely, inventor of the undergarment Spanx,** wanted to be a lawyer but failed the LSAT twice. She went on to sell fax machines for seven years when she finally came up with the idea for a controlled undergarment.

Believe that there is more out there that belongs to you but it is simply waiting for you to grab it. Even if you don't have access to it directly, believe that you will meet the right person to grant you access to those great things. Don't give up on yourself.

Step out and try Something New

In the area below, write your name with your dominant hand. Feel free to use your best handwriting. How does it feel? Comfortable? Easy? Confident?

Now write your name with your other hand? What are the feelings you have writing it with your less dominant hand? Uneasy? Shaky? Awkward? Insecure? Those feelings may be true, but notice something else. Did you feel yourself having to pay attention a lot more than you did while writing with your dominant hand? You had to focus and put more concentrated effort into it this time. In time, if you continued to write with your less dominate hand, you'll get better and better and you'll find your confidence.

Dominate hand	Less Dominate hand

That is what it feels like when you jump out on faith. When you're in your comfort zone, you do things with ease, but even though you feel insecure and uneasy when you step outside of your comfort zone, it causes you to focus and pay close attention to what you're doing. Soon enough it'll become easier.

Jump, and your wings will grow. Trust the process!

☑ Nugget Notes

iPad 🛜   —   100% 🔋

9:01

Ayers Flow

Do not ask God to guide your
footsteps if you are not willing to
move your feet.

– Anurag Prakash Ray

OK

> **slide** to unlock

CHAPTER SIX

Assist in your Own Rescue

Faith without putting it into works is like putting batteries in a remote control expecting the television to automatically turn on. It won't work. You still need to push the power button.

I used to operate that way. I would pray to God for something not knowing that there was work for me to do as well. I'll never forget the parable that someone shared with me that said, "If you're sinking and people float by in a boat you have to swim as hard as you can to the boat for them to even pull you up. You have to assist in your own rescue."

We often pray for the boat, but we hardly ever swim to it when it comes by. Even when you've tried to swim and failed, you have to try again. I've learned that God is answering our prayers but we have to do our part.

Get out of jail card

I remember thinking that I could not believe this was happening to one of "us." My older sister who was just like me is actually in jail. This was her first time being behind bars. She had been picked up for driving without a license in addition to some minor misdemeanors. I got the phone call that she was arrested and needed bail money. My mother was able but not willing to go through this again since she had been down a similar road with my brother.

As tears streamed down my face, I picked up the big yellow phone book. I flipped the pages erratically looking for bail bondsmen. I placed call after call to all the businesses that I felt could help get my sister released from jail. I dialed the last number with a knot in my stomach feeling overwhelmed and nervous that this was my last option. The woman on the other end gave me the same answer as all the previous bail bonds businesses. We needed a large amount of money or we needed collateral such as my mother's house in order to bail her out. I was helpless.

I went into the bathroom and locked the door. I fell to my knees in front of the toilet and began bawling my eyes out. I cried out to God to help me in this situation because in my mind I had maxed out all of my options. I felt completely alone and I hadn't been in a position like this one before.

A calm presence fell over my body. Just as peacefully as ever, I heard in my spirit, "Wipe your face, get up, and go back to the yellow pages." My logic kicked in and I argued with myself that I had already flipped through each page and called every bail bondsman it offered. Nonetheless, I believed what I heard and I followed my spirit.

I opened the book back up to the same familiar pages but this time to my surprise I noticed one that I hadn't seen before. I had missed a page! I calmly dialed the number and the customer service representative told me everything I needed to provide, which was significantly easier to get than what all the other businesses had told me. I had everything I needed to get my sister released.

Looking back on that dramatic event in my life, I learned a few things:

1.   Listen to your spirit. God speaks to everyone in a way each can understand His voice and presence. Trust your spirit when it's speaking to you.

2.   Faith without works is dead. Many times we pray for something and expect so much while we sit there and twiddle our thumbs. God can make things happen when we work for them. I prayed to God to help me but after my prayer I got right up and put in more work and achieved my ultimate goal.

3.   Faith (or belief in something that you see no evidence of) and logic are like oil and water. They simply don't mix. Logic told

me that I had done all that I knew to do. Logic said to stay on the floor crying out to God. Faith, however, is the force that caused me to believe His voice when I heard "Wipe your face, get up." Again, faith without works is dead. Faith with no action behind it doesn't work. My faith could have believed in what I heard but it was the action of going back to the yellow pages that caused it to work. You will either have faith or you will listen to logic in life.

The problem with logic is that it deals mostly with evidence. Logic looks at your past and makes a decision based on it. Logic looks at your current surroundings and bases a decision upon it. Faith, on the other hand, is a belief without evidence. Faith looks beyond your current atmosphere and circumstances and says regardless of the pain you feel today, you are able to move beyond it. Faith looks over your past and says even though you were born into those circumstances and grew up in that neighborhood; it has no bearing on what your future looks like. I strongly encourage faith because it also feels good. It feels good to dream about something that could be. It feels good to temporarily get outside of your current situation and live in your dreams for a while. In addition, faith becomes a tangible force. It's energetic and magnetic and it will become real if you are consistent with what you believe for. Faith is your first step; action is your next. A great example of this comes from my mother.

Mom on her graduation day!

She is a prime example of never giving up because of your current circumstance. There's always more out there for you!

My mother was born in Lynwood, California in close proximity to Compton, a very well known urban city just outside of Los Angeles. She was born into a surrounding that many would classify as a small town with small thinking. Her parents, although smart and great people, weren't the types to get out and travel much. When my mom was a child, she made a conscious decision that she didn't have to become a statistic or product of her environment; rather, she could flourish and thrive in a world far beyond Compton. My great-grandmother is the one who would purchase kids' National Geographic magazines for my mother to read. There, she learned so much about a huge world outside of her immediate surroundings. She learned about animals in other parts of the world. She learned about cultures outside of what she knew. My mom became acclimated to living outside of the box, which wasn't so common where she lived.

With so many examples around her of people who were born and raised in her town who never left, Mom believed things would be different for her, and she later proved that theory right. Her belief caused her to make a decision that became a tangible force in her world.

Though she has been through a tremendous amount of painful events, my mother's belief in her potential kept her going. Sometimes knowing that life has much more to offer keeps you moving for better. Through the power of belief, not only was she able to first finish college and obtain her Bachelor's Degree, she continued to reach further and got her Master's Degree! Today, she is an executive at the company she works for and is doing extremely well for herself. It amazes me to look at her story. I saw her past. I knew where she had come from. I saw firsthand, the trials that she had to conquer, but it wasn't enough to stop her. It wasn't enough to keep her stagnant. She is the primary reason that I believe all things are possible and obtainable. She assisted in her own rescue.

Becoming Familiar With Your Inner Voice

For the next week, try waking up in the morning and being absolutely still. Don't grab your phone and scroll through social media. Don't read emails or text messages. In fact, try not to talk to anyone in your household for the next ten to fifteen minutes. Sit with yourself. Quiet all the outside noise of what needs to be done that day. After consistently practicing this, soon you'll become more familiar with what your inner voice is saying. You'll become more in tuned with that voice and what it says to do and not to do.

The more familiar you become with your inner voice while you're still, the more familiar you'll be when you go throughout the day and hear that voice. One of the most powerful things is to be in an environment full of noise and still be able to hear your inner voice for guidance. It's a key component to making decisions in your life.

Record your progress and write it down! You'll love the progress you make!

CHAPTER SEVEN

Belief works for you or Against you

Do you know what it's like to walk into a room full of people and it gets silent the moment you enter? The tension is usually so thick that you can cut it with a knife. Have you tried walking into a church or temple where immediately you feel a calm presence? But how can you feel something that is intangible? Many people would argue that words are intangible but I disagree with that.

After many years of getting to know myself, and having silent conversations with God, I had built up such a belief that all the things I would speak would become tangible. There was such strength in what I would say that I could feel it in the air.

I would get to the point where I would prove it to people. Just like the story I told you earlier when I was running late for the movie screening, I claimed my favor spot and got it! I would pull up into a packed parking lot with no spaces available and say out loud, "I need my parking space to open up right now!" The key, I believe, is the conviction I had in my voice and the knowingness that this was my space that was becoming available. It seemed to happen like clockwork. I would drive up and a car would be pulling out of the best parking spot in the lot. My husband and I would laugh because it became so ridiculous how immediate this would happen. I would just tell him that it was my "favor spot." I would also tell him to start confessing his parking spaces and sure enough he would have the same results that I did.

That isn't where our "luck" ended, though. I would speak all kinds of things into existence and was proven right each time something happened in my favor. I was favorable! You can speak things out and they will manifest! Favor, connections, finances, resources, and so much more!

When I was in my teenage years I would sit in my sister's car by myself. I would lean the passenger seat all the way back so that I had a great view of the open sky. This was during a time that I came to really know God for myself without anyone ever telling me his or her thoughts and opinions of Him. I figured I would "test" Him to see if He would really communicate back with me.

For hours I would say things like "God, if you're real, send three birds directly across my path right now," or "Send a red car down this street." More often than not, what I would ask for would happen. I like to think of it as a game that God and I would play to get to know one another; Him, to see if I would believe Him, and me, to make sure that I could indeed trust Him. All those times and conversations would prove to me exactly who God was. He built my confidence in a way that no Bible or spiritual person ever could. It was my own experiences that taught me the power of speaking things out and God answering. It had gotten to a point that I simply knew that I was "different," but not in a boastful way. Just in a way that I had tapped into my inner power in a way that a lot of people around me had not done yet. Maybe God felt that if I were bold enough to ask, I was able to handle what I was asking for. Therein lies the key to many of my life's stories.

In those days I woke up with expectation. I would keep my eyes open for special blessings that were just for me. I remember being locked out of my house a lot because I'd lose my key very often. I would leave school and go to a friend's house and we would end up being there all day into the night. I would walk home at night hoping that someone was home because I didn't have my house key. Sometimes I would have to sit on the porch and just wait patiently for someone to arrive. Even though I hated the idea of sitting outside in the pitch dark with no entertainment or no one to keep me company, I did like the idea of spending time alone with God. I'd look up into the stars and ask Him a question. I would say, "If you can hear me, let a shooting star fly by." It might be five minutes or even twenty minutes of time lapsing but sure enough a beautiful, bright shining star would shoot by in the dark covered sky. I would be elated because I believed the gift was just for me.

But let's not make the mistake of thinking belief is always working for us in a positive manner. Sometimes, without even knowing we're doing it, we're calling the things that we don't want into our lives. Sometimes we think we are being positive when that is far from the case. For instance, you might constantly say, "Whatever I do, I can not be late again." Because of the energy being put behind not being late, you'll end up being late anyway. Instead, change your language and your belief will follow. Say things like, "I will be on time today," or "I'm always on time wherever I go." Statements like that will soon captivate your belief. In the book, The Power of Your Subconscious Mind, Joseph Murphy PH.D. states, "The law of your mind is the law of belief. This means to believe in the way your mind works. To believe in belief itself. The belief of your mind is the thought of your mind. That is simple. Just that and nothing else. All your experiences, events, conditions, and acts are the reactions of your subconscious mind to your thoughts. Remember, it is not the thing believed in but the belief in your own mind which brings about the result."

You must understand that whatever belief you have about anything is what you're giving the power and the permission to enter into your life. Stop focusing on not getting sick, not getting married, not having enough money, not receiving love. If you begin to focus on the opposite, your life will change in a drastic way. Start saying that you do have everything in abundance. Say that you are great at what you do. Say that people enjoy being around you. Consistently think on these things, say them and write them down. The conviction alone will seep down into your belief system and the universe will have no choice but to bring it to you.

You may wonder why I use the term "universe" which is understandable. This is not to take power or credit away from God, but just a way to acknowledge that God is in everything. If you've created something with your own hands, it now has the essence of who you are. The universe is something created by God himself and works with the intention that God created for it. Just like He created Earth to have its own laws and seasons, He created powers within the universe that we must acknowledge and take advantage of.

There are distinct abilities that we have that involve the laws of the universe. There are forces such as the power of words and beliefs that will create movement in your life whether you accept that or not. If you come to this understanding right now, you have the rest of your life to enjoy the privileges of what come along with knowing your power. If you are bold enough to ask what you want from life, be in expectation to receive it!

Change your Language

I've frequently had to revisit my language and adjust some of my words that I didn't know could be doing more damage than good in my life. I want you to think about phrases you say often or thoughts that run through your mind often. Re-evaluate them just to make sure you're putting the important emphasis on the right words. Your intentions might be correct but your emphasis might be placed on the wrong words.

Belief can either form your words or your words can form your belief. If you've grown up in a loving household and all of your life you state that you came from a loving home, you'll believe that to be true. However, if you state that you had a terrible childhood and an unloving family, at some point you'll believe that to be true regardless of the facts.

Belief shapes our perception and perception shapes our reality. Change your language to form a more positive perception and your outcome will align accordingly. The importance of changing your language is that whatever you focus on will magnify.

The Difference

Do NOT say: "I will not have a nightmare tonight."

Do Say: "I will have a great and positive dream tonight."

EXERCISE

....

....

....

....

....

....

....

....

....

....

....

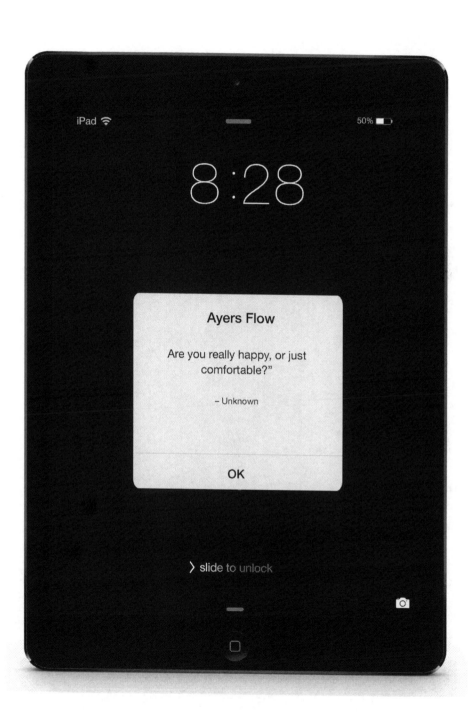

iPad 📶   50% 🔋

8:28

Ayers Flow

Are you really happy, or just
comfortable?"

– Unknown

OK

❯ **slide** to unlock

CHAPTER EIGHT

Beyond 5 Miles

One of the hardest things to do is change the way you think. Where I grew up, people thought that the world is too big to change or that they were too small to make any changes to it. That couldn't be further from the truth. Unfortunately far too many people fail to understand the power that resides inside all of us. The power inside of all of us is like a seed. For some, their seed lies there dormant and unaware of the potential it has to grow, while others may water their seed and shine light on it causing it to be stimulated and show some form of growth everyday. This is what I want you to accomplish with your seed of power.

For a long time I was only shown the safe way to live. I was always told that getting a good education was the way to go, and that college following high school was my way be prosperous. I had no examples of entrepreneurship around me so my only choice was to take a long look at those people who had good jobs and not-so-good jobs. Going that route, although good for some people, is the safe way to go in life. Then you have the risk takers. There is an incredible force that works in your favor when you decide to take risks. All of the risks I've taken were based on my belief that I could accomplish anything. Even if things weren't going to work out the way I had intended, something awesome was going to come from the decisions I had made.

I have a tendency to jump right in when I have the desire for something and allow my wings to grow as I'm falling. I've learned a tremendous amount about myself, about God, and about how the universe works just by jumping and believing it would all be okay in the end. It has taught me that favor works most for people who are already in the game. I usually tell people to just begin an action and something happens from there. We should have tremendous enthusiasm for the goals we are trying to attain. What does this mean? The vision should be so big that we get butterflies in our stomach because of the adrenaline within us. That's how big our belief should be.

Someone once said to me, "People have a tendency to get stuck in the five-mile-radius life. They go to work within five miles of home. They only dine at restaurants and go shopping within a five mile radius of home." Typically these are people who have gained a comfort in knowing that they have control over most aspects of their life. There is a comfort in knowing that every two weeks there is a payday and your check will be the exact amount that you are expecting. There's comfort in knowing that each morning on your way to work, you're familiarity with the flow of traffic is such that if you make a right-hand turn, you will get you to your destination at the exact time that you expected.

I understand that people living this type of predictable lifestyle are controlling so much of their life that there isn't a need to be afraid of goal setting because generally their goals just aren't that big. Their goals will likely be attainable or predictable and totally within their own reach.

I want to make it clear that this isn't a judgment toward anyone who chooses to live his or her life safely. I know plenty of people who live this way and are content with life, including my own mother. I often laughed with my mom about how safe she lives her life. She likes to know page by page how her life looks and possibly what it will look like next week. She is a planner and a logical thinker. Although she plays life safely, her payoff has been huge!

But just like my mother, there are people who have a master plan but still wish to step out on faith a little more. There is a side that yearns to know what it feels like to go after your dreams and passionately believe in them to come true. I'm an advocate of people who make wise decisions but also take leaps of faith knowing that God will catch you. Those are the people that I want to reach. I want to talk to you because I know what it feels like to yearn for it and actually move toward it. God is on your side. The universe is on your side. Belief is on your side to get things done.

A few years ago I made the transition from being a stay at home mom to the world of broadcast journalism. What a huge leap that was for me! I just decided one day that the world needs a positive voice for people with great inspirational stories to tell that should reach the masses. I had no experience on camera so I decided to take a hosting class to sharpen any natural skills that I had. Soon after taking classes I still had no direction but rather than sit and wait or go back to the comfort of staying at home, I decided to move in a direction. I didn't know the exact direction I was moving in; I just chose any direction in hopes that it was the right one. Well, today I don't believe in a "right" direction. I believe that the right intention mixed with any movement will get you to a destination meant exactly for you and your life.

Before long, things started happening for me. I noticed that the more I moved, something moved towards me! I didn't know how I would achieve my dream of becoming a host but I just believed in the steps that I was taking. More than anything I believed in myself and I believed in the power that I had. I'm sure my skill has had something to do with what I have accomplished, but I've dreamt big dreams, and more importantly, I believed in the moves I was making. It often didn't make sense for people who were watching my journey.

How did this girl come out of nowhere with no journalism degree and start interviewing people like she was an expert in the field? How did she skip over the "necessary" steps and begin covering red carpet events? There are no forces in the world that match the phrases "I am", "I will" and "yes." When you make the decision to have a definite "yes" in your mouth and you believe without a shadow of a doubt that it will happen, it has already happened in the spiritual realm and now it will take whatever time needed to manifest itself in real life. Just like the green light signal when you pushed the button at the stop light, the belief is the signal button that you push to bring your truest desires into your life. And now you must wait for the process happening behind the scenes to finish. Finally, the light turns green and you can begin to walk in it.

☑ *Nugget Notes*

11:01

Ayers Flow

Life is 10% what happens to
you and 90% how you respond.

– Unknown

OK

❯ slide to unlock

119

CHAPTER NINE

When The Rain Falls

Simply because you're alive, there will be bad days and even bad periods of time. Sometimes there is nothing that you can do about it, but the way you handle it can make all the difference in the world. Hard times are painful but in the grand scheme of things we learn and grow from them all. Dolly Parton says, "Storms make trees take deeper roots." I know this to be true from my own life experiences.

The Life Changing Phone Call

It's after ten o'clock at night and my mother is usually asleep at this time, so why is she calling me? Those were my exact thoughts as I was sitting in the passenger seat while Robbie was driving the car. We had decided to take a little drive around a nice neighborhood that we were considering moving to with our twins who were two years old at the time.

All I remember is dropping the phone after my mom told me that my brother had been shot and was in critical condition. Robbie took the phone and handled the rest of the conversation. We immediately drove to his parents' home to drop our girls off and the whole way driving I didn't quite know what to do with myself. I remember praying first, then I texted a handful of people asking them to pray as well.

After picking up my mother and stepdad, we took the long drive to the hospital. It was dark and complete silence filled the car. I was pretty sure we were all having the same thoughts. *Will he be alive? Will we be able to see him once we arrive? Can we pray over him and God miraculously work things out in his favor?*

I couldn't believe I was about to experience the exact scene that I had seen in so many movies. Usually the family is sitting anxiously in the waiting room, biting nails or consoling each other with warm hugs that said, everything will be okay. This definitely wasn't the case when we arrived. This was real life and it was only about to become more real.

We had a few friends who had met us at the hospital and when we arrived a few staff members immediately guided us into a small room. I sat next to my mom. We both knew the outcome just by the look on the doctors' and sheriffs' faces. I sat in amazement and couldn't quite make out all the words the officer was saying as he explained what happened, but suddenly I heard, "I'm sorry, but he didn't make it."

My heart dropped, but for multiple reasons. My mother was visibly shaking and I wanted so badly to jump inside of her soul and quickly bandage her open wounds. I wanted to wrap her in my arms like a baby and hush her pain away. I just listened to this man tell us that her only son was murdered a couple of hours ago. Her oldest child was gone and we couldn't see him. Since I had two children of my own, I could only imagine the agony she felt at that moment.

The feelings of disbelief, pain, and confusion stayed with me for a while. It was such an unfortunate situation and I'm quite sure I had never felt a gut wrenching pain like that ever before.

Arthur, Me, Robbie

When we left the hospital, the car ride home was of complete silence. All of us were in complete disbelief. I couldn't really sleep that night, as I had to cope with what was now reality. I wouldn't see my brother Arthur in this lifetime ever again.

Some time that week I remember feeling sad of course, but there was a sense of purpose that came over me. Not my purpose, but my brother's purpose. There was a deep comfort in feeling as though he had already served his purpose here on earth and that he was now being called home because of that fact.

There again is the knowingness, the sheer belief I had that this was the way it was supposed to be. My philosophy is simple for things like this. The earth is turning counterclockwise. Everything on earth is also turning counterclockwise with the flow of the planet. Have you ever heard of the earth coming to a complete standstill and reversing its rotation to move clockwise? That would be against the purpose of what it's meant to do, right? Similarly, we are meant to go with the flow of the earth. There is a purpose for everything that happens. But once we decide to come to a complete halt and reverse our emotions, feelings, and resistance against the flow of what's naturally happening, we are now going against the grain of purpose. Life has a way of putting us back on top again. The movement of the flow we're going in has a way of circulating to get you out of your current situation, but so many of us go against the grain and resist moving along because we are going through something uncomfortable at the time and choose to stay in it for a while. Just know that you can get through any situation in a healthy manner if you have the right frame of mind. Don't allow yourself to get stuck in a place of denial or discomfort when hardships happen. Take some time to think it through, breathe, and know that it will pass and ultimately you will come out on top.

When my brother passed away, it would have been easy to go against the grain and be upset with God or life itself. It would have been easy to be adamant about being sad or harnessing pain, but I chose to go with the flow of life and believe that purpose was moving right along—as it should. I'm not saying this as though it's easy to do, I know that it isn't, but life tends to help you move along the more you move in sync with its purpose.

Many people looked at my mother and me as though we were extremely strong for going through our grieving process as quickly as we did. Don't get me wrong; this is still one of the most painful situations that we've ever gone through; my mother especially. This was very reminiscent of something she had been through years ago.

My mother grew up as the eldest child of three, to my aunt Penny and my uncle Steven. Ironically I had never really known my uncle because he was also gunned down when I was just under a year old. This was probably the first time my mother had experienced real unparalleled pain in her life. The death of her younger brother was probably the same jolting pain I felt when I lost my brother. To think, she was reliving this traumatic experience once again but through her only son is really tragic.

Although this was the second time my mom's life was altered in this way, she had gone through so many ups and downs that she was now my prime example of being optimistic and believing in something positive again.

I have personally watched her pull herself out of seemingly impossible situations and set her back on top. I have watched her continuously climb to new heights when I'm sure many people had already count-ed her out. She is the single most pertinent reason that I believe in all things being possible.

People contact me all the time with their problems or challenges. I never feel like it's impossible to resolve these issues. I don't believe in excuses that validate people giving up on themselves. I hardly ever feel sorry for people but I do empathize with them. Usually I can see past their situations. I can see that there is a light at the end of their very dark tunnel even when they can't. There's not enough time for two discouraged people to be in a dark and lonely place. One has to put on the vision binoculars and see that there is a way out. I don't choose to join pity parties, although I understand them. We're human. My motto is that "It's okay to cry, but just for a moment. There's work to do!" Discouragement, loneliness, fear, and anger are welcomed to visit us but they certainly can't take up residency! That would be an open invitation to allow you to be bitter and angry and scared of life. Try and get your emotional house as full as you can with belief and the family members thereof. That way you can begin to feel as though all things are possible in the world. You can feel happiness and true joy from within.

If you take a second, think back to the beginning exercise in this book that asks you to inhale positivity and exhale doubt and fear. Those are practices that invite the right things to fill you up. That exercise is literally training your mind to accept all great things to live within you and consciously evicting the negative things that no longer serve you. It's a powerful way to live—and it's life changing.

All things work together

Think about the last painful thing that you've gone through that you haven't quite gotten over. Maybe you're still unsettled about it. Perhaps you're angry, frustrated, unhappy or sad about it. Feel the emotion that you felt behind that event. Close your eyes and acknowledge that it happened. Now, if you can, think about at least one positive thing or emotion that came from it. As an example, maybe you were laid off of your job but the positive outcome is that you started a business. You probably wouldn't have had the nerve to quit the job on your own so it probably turned out to be a good thing after all.

1:15

Ayers Flow

Don't follow your dreams;
live them.

– Unknown

OK

❯ slide to unlock

CHAPTER TEN

So you Believe, Now What

So here we are! You get it! You understand that you are the most powerful being on the face of the earth. Yes you! You no longer doubt that you have the ability to make whatever you desire come into your life. Now what? Well, now it's time to apply it.

Have you ever heard the catchy phrase "Common sense isn't so common"? I have finally gotten to a place where I completely understand what that means. Just because you know what to do doesn't mean that you will do it. Many of us want to be great, healthy, fulfilled, intelligent, wealthy and positive but we can come up with hundreds of reasons why not to the things that will get us to those goals. Remember, everything you want to be and desire to have begins with your belief. You absolutely must become more conscious about the thoughts you have and make sure they are in line with your truest desires. Keep several things in mind as you move forward in your new awareness about your power of belief:

1.   Invite positivity and greatness into your life by taking a moment to physically breathe in all the goodness you want to experience.

2.   Be conscious of your language, remembering to put emphasis on the right thoughts and not the negative thoughts. What you focus on will magnify.

3.   Even through tough times, go with the flow and try not to resist. Accept what's happened and continue to move with life's purpose. You will always come out on top by living this way.

It's time to take action! Choose one thing that you want to focus on that you wish to see brought into your life. Put your mind on it and think positively on it. Your next step is to take an action toward that thing. Even if you think it was a misstep in the wrong direction, something positive will still come from that as a reward for being bold enough to take a step in the first place, so you can't afford to be afraid.

Fear will limit you. Fear should be acted upon, meaning if you feel it, acknowledge it and instantly do something to counteract that feeling. For example, if you're afraid of bees, go to the Internet and look up as much information as you can on bees. Find out why they sting, what sets them off, what they eat, how they interact. That is the way to conquer the very thing you're afraid of.

Even as I write this book, I still battle fear. Yes, me—the one who is speaking to you about belief and the power of it! My fear of writing my first book has brought about many battles. Fear of the unknown, fear of my next steps, and not knowing anything about the world of publishing has caused me to water my seed of power also. But the very things I feared, I am conquering day by day. It's very easy to say, "I'm writing a book!" but what comes next? Now there's an expectation to complete and publish the book and get it into the hands of people to read what I've written. That was a very difficult thing to grasp but as you sit here today, you are reading the "fruit" of the "seed" I had to continuously water.

When I first began writing, my voice of doubt was saying, "You're not an author. You may as well stop." Well thankfully I know better. Thankfully I know that I am what I believe I am, and I am an author! I didn't know the first thing about publishing a book yet you sit here with this book in your hands reading it. That is a testament to my belief system! That is also a prime example of the unspoken language that has manifested itself in real life.

There is an innate desire within you. I call it the little commercial that God showed you a long time ago. That desire or dream tugs at you and pulls at you to accomplish it. Once you've gotten yourself aligned with that dream, I wholeheartedly believe that you can lead it to where you want to take it. If your dream is to be a singer, follow that dream and begin to put yourself around the environment of singers. Sing as much as you can. Once you're in the realm of it, lead it. Direct your own path! Begin to go out on auditions for background singing, schedule meetings with talent managers. Do everything you know to do in order to lead that dream where you want it to go. The same is true for whatever field you might be interested in.

No one person is better than another. We all have the ability to lead our dreams where we desire them to go. Become qualified in your field; in fact, become over qualified with knowledge to make yourself as valuable as possible. Use your talents and persistence to become a key player in your field. All the while, be aware of your power. Make it a force in your life to where it becomes evident in the lives of people around you.

1, 30, 60, 90

Start now!

What's the dream in your heart? Start moving towards it today. Write down your plans and any actions moves that will help you with focusing on it. Believe in yourself and find others that believe in you as well. Stay motivated, you've got this!

When I was younger someone helped me create a 3-month plan for myself. It is the most effective way to visualize where you will be using small goals to get there.

Below, create goals in 30-day increments for yourself. What can you do beginning day 1 that will get you motivated to move? What is the big goal you want to reach in 30 days? In 60 days? In 90 days? Every day in between should be attainable things that you do to reach those big goals.

30 DAY GOALS

60 DAY GOALS

90 DAY GOALS

Ayers Flow

People inspire you, or they drain
you—pick wisely.

– Hans F. Hansen

OK

> slide to unlock

CHAPTER ELEVEN

Birds of a Feather

I want you to begin making plans and goals for your life. Many people live by default without making real intentional conscious decisions on what their plans are. There are so many reasons we're told to keep good people around us and stay away from troublemakers and negative people. Here's a story that serves as a good example of why.

CON 2 CEO

James was the class clown and the troublemaker in school. He didn't have too many friends but the ones he hung around were not high achievers either. I'll never forget the day James' friends dared him to steal the luxury car belonging to one of our high school counselors, Mrs. Brown. He just refused to stay out of trouble and eventually he got expelled from school. Years after graduating I ran into a few friends I used to go to school with and James came up in conversation. They told me he had gone to prison for some crazy crime he had committed. It was sad but I wasn't surprised. He had many years of experience getting in trouble for his actions.

Several years later, I pulled into a gas station near my old high school. A really nice car was in front of me, and the license plate read "CON2CEO". I laughed to myself because of how clever that was. I thought to myself, Wow, whoever drives this car must have an interesting story. I thought it was bold to broadcast to the world that you were once a convict and now a CEO of a company.

The driver of the car walked out of the convenient store of the gas station and started pumping his gas. Since I was waiting directly behind him, we caught each other's attention. I couldn't believe my eyes. Is that James? I asked myself. Yes, it was! He must have seen all the expressions on my face because his eyes got big as if he recognized me too. As he waited for his car to fill up with gas he walked over to my window to say hello. I was in shock watching him walk over. Here's a guy that I had only known to be a troublemaker. Last I had heard, he was locked away in jail for doing something silly. Now he's clean cut, dressed in nice clothes, and pumping gas in an awesome car that was definitely more expensive than what I was driving!

"James!" I shouted when he got to my window. "How are you? Where have you been?" I asked as if I didn't know.

He was open and honest about his past troubles that put him behind bars. He said that during his last year of being in jail he started studying real estate material. He became fascinated with it. When he was released he made a few connections in that industry and slowly worked his way up. He was modest about not quite being where he ultimately wanted to be but he attributed his success thus far to God and the people he surrounded himself with. His two favorite places were the gym and the office where he worked. He met a few very successful people in real estate and asked if he could help them with what they needed and in return he could learn as much as he could about the business. He told me that if you hang around millionaires long enough, you pick up the habits of millionaires. He was well on his way to becoming one.

My husband and I always tell our two little girls to align themselves with people who are constantly working toward great goals. These types of people will always find a way to make things possible and not give excuses instead. Similarly, they'll find ways for their friends to succeed. There is a tremendous difference in having believers around you versus naysayers. Naysayers will give you a way out. They will allow you to remain comfortable. In fact, they are uncomfortable when you start to make successful changes in your own life. The phrase "misery loves company" is not just a catchy thing to say but it is a dominating reason to stay away from people who don't believe their own visions. If they can't see their own, what makes you think they can see yours? It's a dangerous place to be.

Believers, on the other hand, can see beyond the horizons. I love talking to mentors and overachievers about life and the possibilities thereof. Oftentimes they can see ways to navigate what may seem like an impossible situation to help you achieve a goal.

My husband Robbie is in consistent personal development. He reads, listens to audio books, and even watches informative documentaries on people who have achieved extreme success. Because my husband is an ambitious person, he loves to take my ideas and enlarge them. He also believes that all things are possible to achieve so I love bouncing ideas off of him. Even if someone who believes in you doesn't agree with your method of getting things done, they'll be able to offer other avenues as ideas.

I have my husband, but you should find two or three people who you feel are very supportive of you but most importantly, are also reaching for their own goals in life. There's something special about people who are always striving for greatness. They are thought leaders, they are challengers, way makers, and ultimately they believe that it can be done. These people in your life have so much to offer. Keep in mind; you also need to be of benefit to them to be a part of their circle.

One of the sole purposes that we've been born here on earth is to serve others. So while we build a network of people who are adding to our lives with support, it is important that we offer our beliefs, support, knowledge, and love right back to them.

It is also important to find people who may be struggling with their beliefs. There are always people who we can help out in life. When you find a way to help someone see the light at the end of a tunnel, that is a blessing. When we bless others, our gift in return is to become more enlightened.

Above all else, acknowledging who you are and the gifts that you have been born with will help you to conquer all fears in your life that would attempt to hold you back from your greatness. The simple truth is that all things begin with belief. Belief is your strongest power and it is your loudest voice that speaks for you when you require the universe to bring you what you need. Always remember, the universe is like a waiter catering to your requests at all times. As you've read by now, belief is the catalyst and it is the undeniable language in which the universe responds to. The stronger you believe, the louder your language speaks for you.

I hope that you begin—or in some instances, continue—to live the best, most intentional spoken language we have on earth: belief.

Testimonies

Often times we forget the blessings that we've received in the past. During the time you've read this book, my prayer is that you've received undeniable blessings that have derived from your beliefs. Write them down! It is so important to look back and be reassured that your power of belief really does work when applied. Feel free to write them below.

Acknowledgements

God

You are, and have always been my rock and first introduction to real peace. My every thought and breath thanks you. The both of us have an understanding that's meant for just us. Please know that I appreciate it and will never take it for granted. I love you.

Robbie Ayers

Sometimes I borrow your confidence in me. I borrow the confidence that you have in yourself! Your faith in me, and support for me has been unreal and a crucial reason why I have grown so much. Thank you for seeing my potential from the first day that we met. You spoke life into me and largely in part due to the man you are; I am the woman I am today. I'm blessed to have you by my side in this journey. For eleven years and counting, I've watched you make incredible strides for your family and I've been amazed every step of the way. As you read these words, my silent prayer is that you can view me in the same way. I love you with my entire being!

Madison & Brooklyn

I learn from you everyday! You're the smartest, friendliest, most amazing kids I know! I love you but equally, I like you. Thank you for not only being my kids but for being my biggest blessings in my life. Continue to be the greatest version of yourself! You're my "Ayers" to the throne!

Mom

Thank you for being the truest example that I know of a phenomenal woman. No one can convince me that superheroes aren't real because I've known one my entire life. Through all the trials and tribulations in your life, you've stood back up triumphantly overcome them all. You are my backbone, my inspiration, and my reason to strive so hard in life to show you that you've done a great job as a mother. I've told you for years that I will make you proud of me. I pray that I've done just that. I love you.

Charles Chiccoa

Probably without realizing it, you've taught me so much in life that I am grateful for. I would brag many times when I was younger that you were the smartest man I've ever known. You could possibly still hold that title. Thank you for exposing me to culture. I believe that's one reason why I'm so smart! Haha. I love you, Charles, and I thank you from the bottom of my heart.

Arthur Hicks (May you rest in peace)

There would be no RaRa without you. The funny, street smart, sometimes rowdy, girl that the world is getting to know is all because I learned it from you. I am your "mini me" and I love it. It's been seven long years since I've seen your face and I miss you everyday. I can hear your voice saying to me "RaRa!! I'm proud of you baby girl". I miss you brother.

My family

Grandma and Auntie Penny, the two of you are truly my solid rock foundation. Sometimes your optimism in life becomes my lenses when mine are foggy. Thank you for every ounce of belief you have in me. I see it and

I appreciate it more than you know.

I feel like I have an army behind me when I think of all of you! You hold me down whether we've seen each other just yesterday or haven't seen each other in years. Your presence is strong in my life. How would I even know who I am without all of you? Leila, you taught me so much in my life and I wouldn't be who I am without your impartation. I love you beyond words. My prayers are always with you. Grandpa, Uncle Michael, Uncle Vandy, Trice, Lakisha, Mack, Lamar, Monica, Anthony, Lil Mike, and all the rest of my family—you are a beacon of light in my life. Each of you has inspired me in ways that you don't even know. I love you deeper than words can express.

My sisters

Ana Nemore and Kendra Segura—I would be lost without you two. We have officially surpassed friendship with all that we've been through. Kendra, we've watched each other grow from teenage girls into women. Thank you for sticking by my side every step of the way. I'm incredibly proud of you. Ana, you're my walking journal. I find it hard to get through even a week without talking to you. The both of you have been with me through thick and thin and I can never express my gratitude enough. Thank you for seeing me as your sister. Maceo & Mavie, I love you!

Brandy Norwood (My God Friend)

The conversations that we have contribute massively to my ability to believe in my abilities. You often say "Belief becomes certainty" and that couldn't be any truer. I can't tell you how many ways you've helped me in my own journey. You truly believe in me and I've gained a lot of confidence because of you. I love you friend!

Koran Bolden

Who knew that the guy on social media would become such a great friend and the ultimate reason I decided to write my first book. Thank you for every ounce of knowledge that you've poured into me.

Phoenix White

For all that you've done for me. God knew the perfect time to place you in my life and I couldn't see you leaving it anytime soon. Thank you for your pure and honest friendship. I truly value what we have.

Kris Williams,

You are a gem. Thank you for being you. You're such a valuable friend to me. I'll never lose sight of that. You're a breath of fresh air! Your belief in me makes me walk with my head a little higher. How can I ever repay you?

The entire Ayers family

Thank you for every ounce of support you've given, Dr. Fred L. Hodge, Jr. & Pastor Linda Hodge-over a decade of wisdom, guidance and strength from you two. Thank you! The Norwood family-Sonja Norwood (my other mom), Willie Norwood (a true father figure), Ray J (you've taught me so much and you don't even know it. Folks family-I love you guys beyond words, Stacey Dillon & Tamara Dillon, Sixx Johnson (anything I need, you never hesitate. Thank you! Diijon Bishop (I miss you everyday. I can only pray that you're smiling down on me), my LPCC family.

Special thank you to:

Quincy Newell, Lisa Price, Shaun Robinson, Christina Milian, Lauren Rodgers, Spectre Plume, Kristen Hamilton

I love you:

My social media friends and supporters! I see you and I love you!

Social Media

t ROBINAYERS

O ROBINAYERS

f ROBINBILLIONAYERS

WWW.ITSROBINAYERS.COM

WWW.UNSPOKENLANGUAGES.COM

81570638R00090

Made in the USA
Lexington, KY
17 February 2018